the Reacquaintance of Love
Love & Selected Poems

YVONNE HAMPDEN
Illustrated by MICHAEL RIVERA

REVISED SECOND EDITION
A YMAH RIVERA PUBLICATION
NORTH CAROLINA

Copyright © 1997, 2004, 2015, Yvonne Hampden
Psuedo: Astariam

ISBN: 978-0-9744086-2-0

All rights reserved. No part of this book may be reproduced or transmitted in any form or by any means, electronic or mechanical, including photocopying, recording or by any information storage and retrieval system, without permission in writing from the publisher or author. For information address:

A YMAH RIVERA PUBLICATION,
yhampden@yahoo.com

Illustrations by Michael Rivera

Edited by Yvonne Hampden and Dan Rustin

Cover photo by Melanie Messina Moe

Layout, Design, and Cover Art by Alexandria Batchelor, Foxee Design. For any graphic design inquiries, please email adbatche@buffalo.com. View full design portfolio at www.foxeedesign.com.

REVISED SECOND EDITION

Acknowledgements

Love and thanks to my spiritual mentor, Nikki Giovanni, who sent me notes telling me to keep going, in my quest to write poetry. With great admiration for Valerie Simpson and her late husband, Nickolas Ashford, who paved the way for lovers wanting to make it work. All of you are Sweet Inspirations in my life.

In loving memory of three Angels

Darlene Thigpen, Lynn Odom-Julius, Ramona Van Duzen-Brown

Foreword

To my past… segments of my life I have been reborn from. Now I have the ability to believe in reincarnation of the soul, what is also called resocialization of the thoughts and ideas. Enabling us to live in many and separate worlds, and to meet by chance, in one. Let us share in the totality of ourselves, and not fear the loss of the other. For I know that you shall always be with me. And, there too, I shall remain.

Yvonne Hampden

Dedication
To the Human Race

List of Poem Titles

Part 1	*Time*	9
	£ove is ...	10
	Presence Is a Virtue!	11
	So as love ...	12
	movingclose to me	13
	time is the distance between two things, people, places ...	14
	Silently	15
	II.	16
	Some Place, In Time!	17
	Message: From me to you	18
	Who I Am	19
	Gonna write to you ... Joy	20
	Our day will come	21
	something spicy	22
	making love	24
	A woman... A man	25
	A love so great!	27
Part 2	*Black on Black*	29
	Person to Person	30
	With everything I feel!	31
	coming home, when's *love* coming home?	32
	Black on black. . . (the city is a ghetto!)	33
	Crying... No tears	36
	Black	38
	tomorrow. . . be my black love	39
	Black ...against my mind	40
	Black Knight in Shining Armor!	41
Part 3	*Caught in the Rain*	43
	Caught in the Rain. . .	44
	Poem II . . .	45
	Poem. . . about johnny doe	46
	...about johnny doe	47

	'Living Together'	48
	If I had one day	50
	…About johnny doe	51
	I am the lost Child!	52

Part 4   *Experience*   55

- What Really? — 56
- separately, i see… — 57
- Capture Me… (a poem for you) — 58
- (Almost like a butterfly) …if i can fly — 59
- Presence sensed a prolonged waiting — 60
- Lightning — 61
- I was never gone — 62
- realizing (thoughts of you) — 63
- Falling out of space — 67
- Slowly, they walk — 68

Part 5   *Space*   71

- In the light of darkness — 72
- Poem… for my brother — 73
- Poem… for my eighteenth birthday — 74
- Tell me my baby ain't sweet — 75
- Women Poem — 76
- A Shadow — 77
- Can i belong to you within this circle? — 78
- How I see her! — 79
- Like the sun rays of God — 80

Part 6   *A Prison*   83

- Freedom… A poem for you! — 84
- A Prison — 85
- A mask unbroken — 87
- For Astariam and Miguel/I — 88
- For Astariam and Miguel/II — 89
- For Miguel (A ROCK!) — 90
- For Astariam …Of bad! — 91

Part 7	***Stay Free***	***93***
	My Enlightenment	94
	…Of Humankind	95
	Poem… Of Humankind	96
	Poem… Jan. 3rd, 1980	98
	planetary ebony	99
	Renaissance	100
	Poem… 11/23/79	101
	Who is God?	102
Part 8	***Wall to Wall***	***105***
	Bathing	106
	Just to be born to you!	107
	The night awaits the dawn	108
	Michael	109
	My baby, Michael	110
	Bob Marley: A Triumph	113
	Brothers, do your job!	114
	the therapist	115
	Ours is a freedom world!	116
Part 9	***Back to Eden***	***119***
	Back to Eden	120
	like birds and butterflies	121
	To Michael with Love	122
	Miguel	123
	The Waiting Game	124
	Loves Face	125
Epilogue		***126***
	True Lover	127
	About the Reacquaintance of Love	128
	About the Author	128

PART ONE

Time

Love is ...

Love is a quiet energy wanting to feel the wind of chance embrace it. A cry of excitement, a tender breath joy gives in love, knowing all too well there is something to be returned.

Presence Is a Virtue!

Presence
              is a virtue
                          'cause it's
only when you're near me
            that I breathe
so well.
            My life comes
                      to a new
height, thinking clearly
                    of you.
                              I dread
                                        your absence,
loneliness (sunders) me
            aimlessly,
I look at your picture and dream daydreams
(I know you so very well...)
reckless desires that go nowhere

waiting for you...

Yvonne Hampden

So as love . . .

So as love
the soul becomes surrounded
by darkness. Trees grow
in an empty mind, leaving
no thought hollow, leaving
no crack empty. On the ground
I stand upon and through
the upward houses which
surround the green.

Love cannot leave
an empty soul
nor reject a giving heart.
Through awareness, the conscious
comes alive and speaks
from the heart
and acts through the body
and walks by the feet of
Our Souls - Giving!

From all loves
you shall not have to lie to me
Or expect that I cannot see
the evil that lies within you.
As a child, you cry out for affection
and I hear you, and I know
that you cannot give what you
don't have.
You've never known to choose
between a mind or a woman
And in depth of my thought
is where I hear you
calling my name:

> "Forever Sun Flower, bloom with my
> unloved heart. For all loves shall
> flower in time."

movingclose to me

6 people across from me
know not who i am
what i do
stare
closely   worry closely
my
next
step
              watch my hands
                            move
who i am what i do
i sit at a table behind
in front   them talking
each other too
'bout woo i am what i do

5 people cross me
my hands stand up
one far from my i's site
slowly   my hand   what i do

          what i do up to u
if u choose   stare   cross me
closely   ly close to me

time is the distance between
   two things, people, places. . .

. . . and we cometogether in the mind

touch your warm hand
    a plump belly a barrier
an unreal glass
two selves toward each other
feel your lips
          poked out behind an unread face
a glass barrier
    built between two people, places, and things.
    built
    between two
       intime
a belly   plump   warm   unreal
    all real
       reality
     caught between time.
two people   caught   between   each other
      i n   t i m e
(aware)
touch
      your mind
         your natural self.

Silently

you test me,
           so silently.
you hurt so cautiously
for the dungeon to reopen.
I see a fire, a blaze of ambivalence
you shutter to make me fall
though, I stand as silently as you,
as tall.
I bear the pain inflicted as part of
the testing.
I bear no heartache to call my own.
I take the beating, boldly, and secure myself
in your pain.
For there in the pain is your love.

In the Dungeon I see Fire.
And again, a shutter, as if to fall us, both,
from the heart-ache you created.
As to shut the door you call your own reopening.
To hurt so carelessly.
A reawakening of the feelings of being
left loveless Once Again.
To take no chances, and
secure yourself,
           In Loneliness…

Yvonne Hampden

II.

Don't give me "things,"
                    baby,
Or, make me depend on you
                          for my survival.
Why do you think of me as
                       weak or small?
Why do you say to yourself
                      that i am as a child, to be
cared for?
                    Fussed over, and disciplined,
that maybe I don't acquire the knowledge of all.
Or, the abundance to want to kill another man,
or attack another soul.

You call me a woman,
because of these judgements.
Fragile, though strong,
Of 'some' intelligence,
       not to conquer the world,
Not without you, at least!

I tell you, I can survive a thousand deaths,
and live my life 2x's over.

Some Place, In Time!

Well, here we are again, you and I,
meeting in one place,
        steppin' in one time.
Aboard some ship, some captain's command.
Keeping as much peace as you and I can.
Within ourselves, spreading it, hand in hand.
To touch on to others a story about some land.
Some time and place,
        In meeting aboard some ship,
We see, face to face.
Some story, hey! I am writing about.
A reality we dream, within our minds,
To destroy some place, in time.

Yvonne Hampden

Message: From me to you

I cannot change the world for you,
I cannot bring you life,
I cannot tell you how to live,
Or ask you not to die.

I cannot bring you happiness,
Or anything else you may need,
Or ask you to believe in God so he may bring you these
          things.

I cannot make you love me,
Or even say that you do,
Or make alive the dreams you hope will come true.

I cannot wash away the bad memories,
The pain in your heart,
Or pay for your debts, which may pull us apart.

I cannot begin to show you or tell you what I mean,
Or give you the power to do these things.

But if I can make you believe only you can,
          Then I can.

Who I Am

Who I am. Protected by this cold world.
They tell me it is love that makes them do
this.
I feel hate.
They fear to let me grow, let me see and feel.
They fear to let me hurt out of love.
They fear that I might turn to the evil they enjoy.
Who I am? Protected in this hollow world,
on this shallow ground.
But I can see them clearly, and I am not afraid.
Who I am. Protected; hidden away.
I can only pretend that I have been there.
Who am I? Protected and feared.

Don't tell me out of love you do this,
Because I feel the hate. And:
Don't tell me you fear my mistakes.
Why don't you love me and let me love?
Why don't you live by me, but let me also live?
Why do you fear that I will learn what life is
And find out the tricks?
And why do you cover me with the stories that you
tell?
Let me learn, let me grow,
Let me love and feel,
Let me be.
Let me live. Let me tell where I've been.

Yvonne Hampden

Gonna write to you... Joy

gonna write to you, love
about the ways in which I feel
about you.
You are my destined future.
Sensitivity lies within you.
A deep felt peace
and freedom seen about you.
Putting pieces of my puzzled self
back into place, one by one, I
begin to understand, through definition
of the self, who you are and what you
are to me.
I am glad that we have chosen each other freely,
and want each other peacefully.
Joy is our destined future,
patience is our present love.

Our day will come

One day, our day will come
And, the tranquility surrounding us
will be, you and I, in a field of daisies.
The warmth of the day, with the sweetness
about us, we breathe the same breath of air.
The sun so bright
Our hearts as one
Our day will come, my love
Our day will come.
Splendor in the grass, laughter
for the sunlight, of joy from our
hearts, from love of our souls.
It will be that we can
never part.
It'll be that we can never go away again.
An untold story in the back of my head.
I reach out to you
for the day that comes to be ours.
That remains with us, for
what it came to be.

something spicy

seemingly,
    i can guess
that you have always been there
for me.
    Watching,
     waiting,
      listening,
to the hollow disguise I've worn
for so long.
     Honestly aware of every
step I have taken to get away
from you,
    wanting
      to come closer.
Can i touch you again one day?
Will i want, forever, with such a longing?

Like when you are here
and when we are one wonderful
thing i do
    to make you so very happy.
forget so much of hatred
of, about paralyzed nights
cold winter days
cold summer days
warning me about you
something like
    what i keep
forgetting to do
    No letter for the
past three days.

    Don't forget
about me for a moment.

Don't let your moments mean
forever.
    You're still angry at me!
Everything is inside of us
only when we're one.
Two separate everything's
    are nothing
without one,
so children can be born.
    Because if not, the
world will end.
    The sun will become
one red hot flame to burn out,
into a blue color, then so
white hot.
    Burn out time!
then no more you or me.
Then we'd have to find
something spicy
    something hot
and juicy, to remind each
other what it used to be like, then
children can be born.

Yvonne Hampden

making love

(laughter)
...and then the realization of knowing
I
       shouldn't be
             in thought that way

about our love,
          having reached a climax.

(more laughter).
...not because it's funny,

but
          because it's so beautiful,
                 and, oh!,
                          it feels

so good.
          I look at you, and we know
          what it's about

Eyes search each other tentatively...

A woman... A man

A man can so deeply hurt a girl.
He can turn her into the cold hungry world.
She'll become useful to men.
The only way she can feel worth something is by being
used by men, being needed by men, being loved by men,
trying to escape the reality of his desertion.
She loved him deeply.

Why so cold? You walk so alone in an unsecured world,
your wound left open.
You make me suffer to see you hurt yourself so.
I want to love you, yet you do not trust me,
you do not trust yourself.
You are afraid of yourself, your hurt feelings.
Of being warm and secure again
and having to face the world alone once more.

Oh! don't be afraid.
Be thankful for every moment of it, and that it lasted
that long.
Because if he left you; said he never loved you,
there was one moment that he did,
he once did. Keep that in mind.

              God Bless You

A woman can so deeply hurt a man.
She can turn him into the cold hungry world;
against the cold hungry world.
He'll punish women every time they make him hurt.
He'll seduce them. He'll look everywhere for his
manhood.
And chop every tree (woman) down to find it.
Once it is restored, he can rightfully live again, love again.
But, he shall live in hell if it is too late.

Do not punish yourself so, young boy.
You have not been fooled, you have asked for too much.
Because your love was so great I ran from you.
Or, you offered me something but wasn't there to share
it with me.
Be thankful for what once was; for what we had.
Oh, don't be afraid.
Be thankful for every moment of it, and that it lasted
that long.
Because if she left you; said she never loved you,
there was one moment that she did,
she once did. Always keep that in mind.

God Bless You

A love so great!

A love so great!
Oh! What we've known, what we've shared.
Thank you, I do.
You've shown me something I've never seen before.
You made me feel a way I've never known I could feel.
You let me see love and life in your eyes, in your heart.
In your heart there is something no one else has.
Something I will only feel in a lifetime.
Thank you, I do!
You made me come to life,
I thought there was no life.
You've made my mind tranquil; you let my soul rest
upon yours.
I've seen heaven,
And your spirit shall live in me always.

PART TWO

Black on black

Person to Person

First
        -think of me as a person,
a total and equal human being.

Then know me as a Man
        and respect me for what I can do.

And when you look at that Man,
        know that he is Black.

Know that I am a Black Man,
        with Power.

Think of me first as a Person,
        Who knows not all of everything
but cares just the same.

And know I am of Love.
        A person who loves you. A Man,
Black Man who cares.

First
        -think of me as a person,
a total and equal human being.

Then know me as a Woman
        and respect me for what I can do.

And when you look at that Woman,
        know that she is Black.

Know that I am a Black Woman,
        with Power.

Think of me first as a Person,
        Who knows not all of everything
but cares just the same.

And know I am of Love.
        A person who loves you. A Woman,
Black Woman who cares.

With everything I feel!

Be for real, my love
be true, alive!
Live while you have life,
with everything I feel for you!
I see and know how much you love me.
And with this trust,
with this fear of rejection, but
with this trust, this new hope,
I know we have each other.
And to believe in ourselves, to be one
with each other. And to give,
to, for, with tomorrow.
Tomorrow is ours my love.
Everything is to be real,
we are real. Love, truth,
all of life, beauty!
With everything I have and hold
Of you, all of you… you are of
my deepest need, of my deepest want and desire.
You are pure, of lasting gold. Pure Gold!
And, to give to the fullest, to give birth,
A seed… a new life, the fulfillment of our love.
Who could ask for anything more precious?
And in being black, with everything I feel in me.
Loving each other in our blackness.
To the ego of the self.
God… in the likeness of God, my love. Finding you, loving
you, what more can I say? Words, so they walk and
talk and see and hear. But what we have my love, with
everything I feel!

coming home,
when's love *coming home?*

When you coming home?
When you gonna be mine?
Daddy, be mine
My black honey
Sweet as cotton candy.
Loving,
    coming home to love me.
Sharing love, and making love.
A Child be born of our love.

When you come home Black love,
I'm gonna love you.
Be mine, you gonna be all mine.
Saving all I've got for you
my fine black honey.
Sweet, as sugar and honey.

When you coming home?
    Black Man.
Gonna love you,
    make love to you.
Gonna be mine. All mine. Mine!
Saving my days, all the worlds,
all the stories.
Be my black honey, be my man, my love.

And tomorrow will be gone,
for the time be now.
So tell me,
    when you coming home Black Man?
Coming home to be mine!

Black on black. . .
(the city is a ghetto!)

    Black on black
Nigger
            squash that cockroach
nigger
            sweat
A thousand hours a day

white honky-
            black bitch
I found a penny
            two cents to save
going home
            rat hole
three in a bed

Black nigger
            cornrows
motherfucker
            in momma's bed.
Hit a number
            blacky
25.00 dollars a month to spend.

Rob a car
            Black Cadillac
Be a man
            Nigger
Save my pride
            get off the line.
Black on black
            I robbed a Cadillac.

Yvonne Hampden

Being a nigger
          pussy giver
Another child on the way
seven mouths to feed
          loving
               my pimp
get 50.00 dollars a day

Walking out - walking in
          poppa don gone away
walk in white Man
          Hide it in the garbage can
welfare check come late this week
Pray we hit that number
          Go to grandma's house to eat.
Black on black
Nigger
          sweat
          tears

pray Nigger-
          Honky
save me this day i get through
Looking for a miracle. Pray,
look at honky pray--Nigger
sucking dick to get his due.

White/Black on white/
trying to be
          I'm blue
Kissing ass
          my white man
I don't know
what i woulda do.
Flunky nigger

Whitey in disguise
I took whitey off
        when he pulled out a
        dime
Look at whitey
    run
Black on black
All around

Suffer
        Cause we've got it all
Nigger
        Blacky, Lazy man!
White honky
        Black bitch
Doing all
        getting none
Honky Nigger
        Pussy giver
Black pride
        Woman pride
Sweat - - -
White on White
        Black on black
Being Black
My Man –
        A thousand hours a day!

Black Man
        loving –
Walking in –
        Black on black!

Crying... No tears

Why so many questions?
>*
>
>*

Because I haven't got the answers.
>*

Why so many lullaby's?
>*
>
>*

Because I haven't the food to feed you with.
>*

Why so many deaths?
>*
>
>*

Because someone must die.
>*

But why so many deaths?
      Why must they die?
Is it only to leave us to suffer?
to cry?
And why is no one satisfied?
      Or is it just a game?
And where are my answers?
      or haven't I been heard?

Is there no one there?
      Is it only my reflection?
And is it me,
      who must answer

To the call, to the questions?
To Life?

What is Life? Or is it life is what it is?

And is there no one there
                but my weak and tired reflection?

Or haven't I been heard?
            Is it just a game?   Then why is no one satisfied?

And, why so many lullaby's?
        so many deaths?
Why must they die?
      *

Haven't I been heard?
      *

Because I haven't got the answers.

Black

With you there are no tomorrows
only the realities of yesterday
'Cause never did I believe
anyone could share my dreams...

...and, I'd love to paint you
touch your soul with my eyes,
each perfect place
        within your face
to measure time and space.

tomorrow... be my black love

Gone so long ago
        far from here.

Meeting my destiny
        meeting you there.

Far - so long ago
        Next to my heart.

Gone - so far away
        From here
        to there
Next to my heart.

        I'll carry you
    just let me love you
        Meeting you there.

From here
        We've walked so far.
    Meeting our destiny
        meeting you there
Next to my heart.

Black ...against my mind

        White dove above blue waded waters
clouded skies against my mind
        misty brown poppas   i color love
against my mind
each life i take no chances but to let you into my world of
                black gold.
waded waters against my mind
        washed don washed all my troubles away
out against my mind f l o a t i n g a w a y

        day dreaming against my mind

well i don't care no chances but to let you into my world of
                black
                gold.

If you let into my world me into my world against my mind

  each life i take day dreaming don washed all my troubles
out against my mind
        let me sail my ship on dry land
above my White dove brown poppas i color love

        i color love each life i take
letting you into my world of black gold against my mind...

Black Knight in Shining Armor!
Dedicated to 44th US President-elect Barack Obama, 2009-2016

You're a prince
           to me,
A knight in shining armor.
Golden, as the night,
           the stars
above your suit,
           your pride
shining bright.
           My Black Knight,
in shining armor.
Proud and agreeable to all
           that is
Real!
I love you! My prince,
           so brown and bold,
A figuration of Gold!

All that is worthless cannot
be known.
           Your intelligence dismisses
all negligence.

You are "my prince"
           in shining armor.
Your silence captures
           my full
attention.
Your awareness makes me
so much more aware.

It frightens me to see you
so near, the truth
an unsaid word too many,
yet you use it without fear.
And stars
           shine above
                    your suit,
Your pride shining bright.
My Black Knight in shining armor,
addressing the realities of life.

Yvonne Hampden

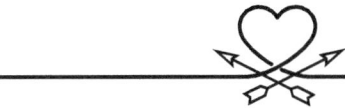

PART THREE

Caught in the Rain...
about johnny doe

Dedication
May petunias continue to grow in the garden of your soul.

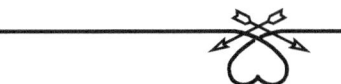

Caught in the Rain. . .

about johnny doe

It rained today
i knew it would
it took from me
all that it could.

I got caught outside
without a hood
and went home soaked
as sick as i should.

I'm trying my best
to die tomorrow
hoping in death
there's not much sorrow.

To go without
a will to write
got no money,
no love in sight.

Instead of dying
with nothing to give
I guess until i get,
i'll just have to live.

Poem II . . .

about johnny doe

smile a joyous day
    and to take the pain away would be
grand.

      to deal with the man
my head can stand the pressure
    but my heart seeks out not to be
used by the female flesh
    but to stay warm
(. . .she also loved me!)

Frankly,
      though, my Johnny Doe
Hurts inside of his pain,
filled himself up with lies,
    he's disgusted with himself,
        Now he's growing up!

Yvonne Hampden

Poem... *about johnny doe*

he hangs up on a drug

i find in him
the world unknown
he toys with life
and dangers shown

fear to him
is unbelieved
to see through him
he's like a tree.

branches hanging
old and dry
but this tree's roots
are sowed and tired.

he hangs up on a drug,
as sun, by time
trying desperately
to find his mind.

...about johnny doe

to turn to God
for thought and need
and in return
do a good deed

letting the conscience
be your guide
to always have him
on your side

to know that
what you've done was right
and in return
feel great delight

no one wants to feel guilty
for what he did
we continually ask God
will he forgive

It's just that a man tries to justify
the things he does
especially when
he believes he'll lose the ones he loves.

Yvonne Hampden

'Living Together'

my booty shaking in your face
i teased you good, then made you wait
you ain't no good anyway
you never do anything you say.
Then you hit me hard and made me cry,
asked for forgiveness, told me a lie.
I hate you, man, you son-of-a-bitch
your ass is skinny, you got no dick.
you think you bad, you think you cool
but you ain't nothing but an ugly fool.
You motherfucker, i saw what you did,
then you tried to hide her under my bed.
I'll kick your motherfucking ass
treat you bad, break you like glass.
suck my pussy you trouble-maker,
kiss my ass you booty-shaker.
finger-fuck me to death, i don't care
making me wet, then bringing me to tears
forget all that "I love you," shit,
everything you say makes me sick.
Go ahead, hit me again - - you fool
hurt me bad - - use me to abuse.
you fucking bastard
it ain't lasting
you tried your best
i did the rest
i cursed and screamed
i made you mean
i led you on
i stuck that thorn
in you, then laid
the feelings' fade
my belly's fat
my children sat

down by your side
they let us slide
still call you dad
but me -- I'm mad
'Cause you ain't shit
but a nigger bitch.
Yeah! now you glad
you silly ass
who you think you are
some superman?
I kicked you out
left you alone
Why ain't you gone?
it's your freedom song.
you're full of shit
you nigger dick
can't nothing satisfy
what you want
so you shoot dope
and make a big front.
I love you though
but you say "So"
can't nothing last
you've had my ass
no pussy left
no cum to bless
said someone's coming
to save us both
you'll try again
but i can't boast
can't talk bad
but have to be glad
'Cause the love we have
has turned us MAD!

If I had one day

If 'i' had one day, and
in that day ' i ' could have
'my' way, if 'i' were invincible
then 'i' would be God.

...*About johnny doe*

Through the process of elimination, I want and have nothing within my presence that does not need you. You are a seed within my very soul, implanted there, without any warning of (it's) awareness.

      At the point of its evolution, which each and every form of humane life shall escalate from. With the proper cohesion of two(2) cells, pro se, you + I will become one. Meet! in some thought; some form of acting/ action.

      The emotions I experience say to me, I can never forget this thought about you. These thoughts of you can never be forgotten.

So much is against me. I am against so much, within myself.

I am the lost Child!

Allah is my present being (existence)
God is my total form (of becoming).
Man is my sanctuary church
in which my altar is placed...

... I am the lost Child
forgiven of being born too soon,
much too soon. I am
more and more of myself, plus less.
Fewer people know me better
than they once thought they could...

. . . tried and tested,
      bought and
           often than enough

found dead
      and buried.

PART FOUR

Experience

What Really?

What really is your game?
What really do you want
from me?

What really can I give you?
What really is your style
of life?

What really can you do?
What really are you hoping for?
What really - me you use?

What really is your game?
What really are you up to?
What really are you trying
to ignore?
What really do you be
so cool?

What really are you so depressed?
What really do you want; need?
What really bag are you in?
What really is your thing?

Really!
And what's it all about?

separately, i see...

something staring right at me
i cannot see,
      a face in an
expression of its unnatural self
Disowning each disguise it
hides behind.

separating, he from she, you
from i, he from it, me
from my.

      Why in each reflection
i see only an image of despair
      Little hope of reaching
nowhere, to the dream of
getting there
      or here, where the
peaceful thoughts shall bring a
reality of happy imaginings.
why, in each reflection, i see
only i, separately.

Yvonne Hampden

Capture Me... *(a poem for you)*

Let me just hear the voice of your soul
The thoughts of your spirit,
                              chasing me.
Capture me...
        the way a bird captures a worm
and eats him.
Suck me under your wing, the
dreamer you are.

Suck me in with your beak.
your thoughts of me
        will suck me in,
the way I want to be.

Capture me...
        the way a dreamer
captures his dreams.

(Almost like a butterfly) … if I can fly

If i can fly,
then i am a bird,
a dreamer, in the sky
of my mind.

where is the love?
the rain?
the emotion?
to be felt at the time of
            decision-making.

With anxious discovery, and
with the fear of the unknown,
can make my peace of mind
become chaotic,
tortured destiny,
future gatherings to be made.

I say that before me, my God
is spoken,
Represented in words.

Yvonne Hampden

Presence sensed a prolonged waiting

Presence sensed a prolonged waiting
Sensed the ticking of a clock
that has always stood still
in time   in time
As though it resented time,
itself.
I watched that clock, though
it was not moving
I listened to the clock's ticking sound.

It was singing a poem that
the story of my heart beat
has written down.
         To understand,
forever, within my mind, the
stood still presence the body
I am in has represented.
As the clock that is not moving,
my arms are reaching out to you.

Lightning

    you
         give
              me
              chills
sent up my spine
like lightning sent from the sky,
you touch my earthly nature
with magic powers
of your soul.
Baby,
        soul!
Baby, you've got soul!
Baby, you've got soul!

you make me wanna dance!
you make me wanna prance!
you make me subject to stance!
because my innocence
                              is!
my innocence is
            knocking against things.
my innocence is
            bouncing
upon walls,
        Up, against
                      things!
Cause,
        you send chills up
                my spine
Of humane
      nature,
          against
              things.
like lightning sent from the sky,
you touch my earthly
            nature!

Yvonne Hampden

I was never gone

IN a search
        everlasting!
continuance,
          permanence
All words of years to come,
years past gone
Still i can touch each moment,
past or present,
        Still,
                      I can reach
each peak,
        of yours,
                Forever.
This love be forever
in my defining of a dance
                    that won't
say, but is a part of my forever soul,
and the longings,
        and the desires,
each reward
        Of riches, priceless amongst
the sun.
        I want you as you are,
I need you as you become,
        Can you say to me,
                don't leave me
as i come and come
        Again in the
same moment, at only
        a different time.
See! i was never gone,
        never, never gone.
Never a lost soul
        were you.
Never will you be.
Keep me always in your past,
Keep me always for the longings,
each past as a longing.

realizing, (thoughts of you)

I want to
          feel myself
kissing
          your lips.
Being so tenderly
          touched
by your warm warm hands.
My body into
          your body,
Real close and warm.
I want your
          lips,
to embrace my face,
up and
down -
          Across!
My neck line
          'needs' -
to feel your hands.
Your hands,
upon my
whole
Body.
          In a place
          of your
                    fragrance.
The close color
          of a flower
against
          your body.
You rubbed up against
          that flower
and took its Odor.
I do Adore you
          that way...

Yvonne Hampden

Reach me!
Stem out as a flower
        to touch
my body.
           I need you!
You've been away so long.
           My life is
almost over. My love has yet to be
born. I am waiting for your spirit.

I think,
        maybe,
         i can
forget you...
If only for a little while,
        anyway.
My memory speaks
of you
constantly,

          Wondering
          to worry.

You are very quiet
lately.
Very moody and
silent in your
voice.
I speak to you with ease...

Will you hate me the way
you say you do,
or could,
if i happen to displeasure you?
My wants
         and needs

                         cannot
be totally fulfilled
by you,
At present.
Your bondage
                              denies me
Any and every part of you.
Who are you
who has done this
to us?
          I continually love all of you
Self: So why are you angry at me?

Do you hit
          upon things?

Do you forget me?
          Do you need
me, still?
          Every emotion
               within you,
                    has frozen.
I think i know only 1/4 of you,
One-fourth of your
               love,
                    No spirit about
you. You only show your concern
towards me.
               I am frightened, are you?
               I feel your
loneliness.
               I am lonely without you.
               Are you keeping busy?
               Why don't
you care for me to know you better?
I look into space,

Yvonne Hampden

                    and i see
every inch of your body.
Your skin so brown, and
            cocoa-buttered.

So soft, so loving...
            Flexible and firm!
I can see you just standing
            there,
waiting to touch me,
            Waiting for
me to undress myself.
            I can feel the
passion + i smell the lust of
your needs.
            So strong the want.

Stay serious that way,
            Because I am
serious about you that way.

I wonder what exercise
you have mastered today.
            I wonder
what flesh of mine you have
expel(ed)
            that thought from
your mind, please baby,
you are mine, still,
            are you?

I wonder, do you miss me?
I wonder, do you seek me?
In ways of what is,
            Write soon.

Falling out of space

to become a part of your forever

my
   love,
all i want
               to do
                   is
                       be
                         with you.
exist between the times
                       of
                        your love
                               touching
                                     me.
Awaken to
   the early
      sunshine,
               all
that is
   within
      your heart,
         your mind,
         your
thoughts leave me
               dazzling about.
i love you
               with a profound
                       base
of Emotion
            escalating
               from realm
to rhythm,
            falling
               out
                   of space
to
            become a part
             of your
               forever.
Be my love, be my man,
                   my love
Be my love, my love,
               love my being. . .

Slowly, they walk

Slowly,
               they walk
into the distance.
Your voice takes
               serious steps
                         forward.
It sounds as though
you have been marching
                         to here.
I feel a beat
          like that of a drum.
March!
Is it the nearness
of tone, in your voice
that has brought me
            to this piece
of paper,
            Reconstructing the mood
you left me in?

Your last letter
            left me marching
in beat.
I still feel the harmony
of that march.

Your *voice* has brought me
to this place.

PART FIVE

Space

In the light of darkness

In the darkness
      of the light
Or, in the light of (the) darkness
There you stand, before me
as a shadow of my self
Searching from without
Searching from within, trying to get out.

Loneliness,
      within the pain
of not seeing you in the morrow
Or, that I may not be allowed
to touch, or make love to you in my dreams
My only hope is to walk outward
the sun. No shadow of hope beside me.

Poem. . . for my brother

Winter washed away
the dreams of past summer days
Morning-early
sunshine
it's all a part of another year,
another growth
Standing there by a window-sill
looking onward the street
Music of your soul singing
for all hope of a new born dream,
forced upon you by some woman-child
And your child,
born for tomorrow
and a brighter day
A reflection/
as a reflection of what is outside
of a window, upon a street.

Yvonne Hampden

Poem . . . for my eighteenth birthday

The years have all blown over
and the decisions of existence
have become mine
Nothing is complete or incomplete
Everything is in the process of completion

Totality is everyone's dream
in deciding to be free from most things
and obligated only to themselves
It seems as though people hate people
within their years of loving the reality

So, today is seen as all in all
everyone strives for perfection
and we are always making choices
as to which way to live and not
to live

Because I know that within
there has to be truth and spirit
to experience life and love
Everybody seeks truth in love
even in denying its spirit in life

Tell me my baby ain't sweet

Melanie strong and able,
find the truth if you remain capable …

tomorrow's dreams are your little foot-steps
walking down the path, going where the rain
has stopped, and where your heart continues to
laugh. tomorrow's dream is my renewal of the past
, is you Melanie, where the sun has turned
yellow like a butterfly or an autumn leaf, or
some magnificent white snow.
Thoughts of you don't have to rhyme or
make me want to bake you lemon pie. But they
do bring me to terms with myself.

deeper than the eye can see…
looking deep inside of me
searching for the ultimate of fantasies, ever changing
its seminarian qualities.
you were born out of ecstasy, reaching for reality,
born to bring me legacy for an intimate chance with
the almighty, creator of you and I.
you bring me hope for a better day, and give me the
strength to find a new way, to dissolve the mysteries
of yesterday and prove the past has relinquished into
ash. to set aside time, to bring you this rhyme, and
to bring out the better person in me, deeper than the
eye can see… looking deep inside of me, bringing
me an ecstasy, lasting 'til eternity…

…Melanie, strong and bright,
don't give up without a fight.

To my daughter!

Women Poem

Once I thought freely
of my ideas,
Yet, that man and child
have swayed me desperately
beyond my nurtured self.

I shall not know the feeling again.
Once you came towards me
with open arms, full of love and
lovely belongings.

I will not
be there any longer, to serve you
I will not come. . .

A Shadow

You had to see me in this way.
Not a shadow.
A reflection of myself upon a wall.
Turn when I turn.
Still when I'm still.
And, shall the Universe control me
in such the same way?
I, to be, reflected as the Universe's Self
upon the Earth.
Not in all ways,
but to always be seen in this way.
The way you turn or stand still.
Shall I, first, feel the need for you to
turn, as toward the sun (the light of the world)?
And, the need of you to stand
on your own two feet.
Must I, first, feel
your love for me? To Reflect, like a
mirror on a wall, my feelings of love for you.
As two planets in the Universe shall be
as ourselves. And, we, to reflect
the image of ourselves, upon ourselves.
So we shall always love.
All ways. . .

Can i belong to you within this circle?

Can i belong to you
        within this circle,
               of space,
Or this space
        within this circle
of belonging within you?
              may I?

How I see her!

Dark eyes/Rivers
           blue as the sun's set
of tranquil stars
           in the ripe of night.
Destiny abounds me
           traveling faces astound
me... Frigid old men, competent of any women's love
           stand still in
tall exposures of the moonlight.

Moon-lit destiny, searching for the answers of time.
How I see thee/how I see her ... ALL MINE!

Yvonne Hampden

Like the sun rays of God

Like the sun rays of God,
each turn of time
The seasons of the sun
I am under a rule
set off heat, setting off light
I may burn away
My love for you pulls me closer

Like the sun rays,
each turn,
the seasons,
I am under
Set off heat
I may burn
My love for you

Of God
of time
of the sun
A rule
setting off light
burn away
you pull me closer

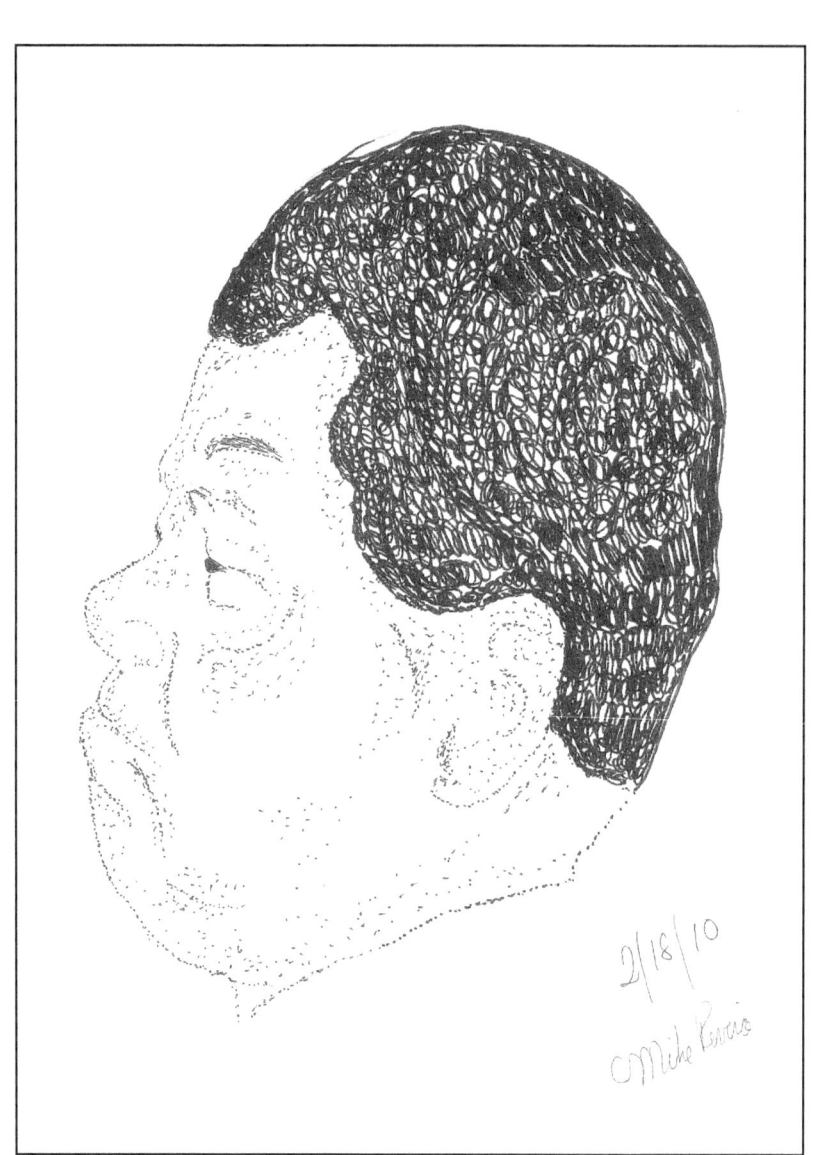

PART SIX

A Prison

Freedom… A poem for you!

To the unchained memories
of living in an atmosphere
created by your own choices.
Decisions made by one mind
and one mind of your own.
Made to save an existence
of value, about you.
Let emotions
        surface
from you, let each memory of life
flow freely,
        from you
Of course,
        I must say,
about the pain of freedom.
'Cause,
        he who chooses to be free
in one way (of most importance),
will also
        be feared in another.
'Cause, to be free,
        is to be
of no expectation of me,
        Of him, nor of yourself.
To be free is
        to be a part of
every partition of motivation.
Every sense of function
        shall come alive!

A Prison

introduction:
                this place

This place of unhappiness, sorrow, and pain
this place, a place of no time and space
filled with nothing but disgrace

this place is no place, no place for you
nor I, for it brings nothing but heartache
to those who are here, they will never survive
they will surely die

For those of you who are
not hip
to this place, take my advice,
stay away if you wanna stay alive.
This Place,
                a place more dead than alive,
All who are here will never survive.
For to enter this place of 'misery longing for
company,' this place of madness, no joy
and filled with sadness,
                you will surely die!
                Mr. Davis

A prison is to be considered
an ugly place of non-existence
where men have been created
into monsters,
and children
should not visit,
'Cause everything is dark and
gray (as the color of your skin),
Black! as,
                like, going to a funeral
and opening a coffin to find a

Yvonne Hampden

body, dead without a mind (or soul).
Though, in prison, a man is found
locked behind a cage, to stampede
and complain,
      and
to think!,
       of causing
some great harm to you,
      implanted
in his brain upon rearrival, in
a society,
      Of people (human, just as he),
who have cooped up in their minds,
as you,
       some non-existing truth,
Living in a non-existing lie,
Not willing to see.

Will you understand
that while his body may be caged
his mind is free?

      Could you possibly
relate to a man who has feared
to know of love,
      as love has always
left him loveless,
As pain has always turned to hate.

So, a barrier is created, of society
against a man, of men
who are left in a voidless world
to be considered non-existing monsters
of timeless time.

     Introduction by Mr. Davis.
     Mr. Davis is a poet; contributor.

A mask unbroken

Behind no mask, of
                a mask unbroken.
No-one can mark the virtue
of a mask, unbroken,
                Or spoiled,
by the true nature of a judgement
past upon a man,
                to "serve" time.
As opposed to time having always served
                        him.
So, this is to the future. A place
that has not, yet, come into being.
A belief of the present to remain
a part of the past,
                so to have captured
a whole day of freedom.
Peace of mind!
                A piece of my mind,
so to let you know exactly where
I am coming from.

I miss you!
        Yes, you,
                MY people!
I miss people.
                MY people!

I miss human beings.
                Having
once been humane
        in their being
Here,
        on this planet
we have called Earth...
                Eternal Universe!

Yvonne Hampden

For Astariam and Miguel/I

as we come
together and connect,
a circle will have been
created between us. As that
circle evolves, the soul as
fire, will rise and be-
come one hot blaze.
Of love...we shall
b u r n ...

For Astariam and Miguel/II

Coming in the midst
of a new beginning,
     of you,
sort of sullen about people.
Burnt crisp of love unmistaken.

The form and shape of words
you take in so easily to define a mind.
So sharply, you achieve a culture of a kind,

Of the people you have chosen, to have a purpose,
Being directed upon your own purpose to survive.

For Miguel (A ROCK!)

You seem so
far alone.
As a rock that cannot show reaction
While a strong cold wave
hits up against it.
So, I have to wonder
about the fear you do not have.
Not willing to tell
about the suspicions you have, within,
about why I have accepted you.

I can't see you at all!
I hate it this way.
Having been pulled out of an existing
time, into a(n) non-existing time.
It's hard to express about a rock.
He's hit upon, with cold waves,
And birds come by to eat off him,
As the sun may give reflection off him.
He's just there, for two lovers to love upon,
to be considered a rock
Without roots, he assumes
he does not need.
I cannot see you Miguel,

Maybe Astariam can,
                      Of course.
I never asked that rock, to know of him.
I suspected his suspicions to be insane,
of me, to know about me.

For Astariam ...Of bad!

I just ought to be
what I'm not
not when I am,
who I what,
        when I is.

I am bad!
        like say,
Damned you yesterday,
today, I don't want to be
that way
        about it.
It's like, the way "I" say.
I'm bad! / off Badness...
        into,
              maybe I'll will it
If i can, what you do
            for me
In return, of myself.
Satisfied,
        to have gotten.

PART SEVEN

Stay Free

My Enlightenment

you enlighten me,
         take away a dull cloud
from my day.
There you are,
A Sun,
         of Stars
Born unto me.
I want the love I endow
from your heart
         to touch my
every emotion
         and reawaken
the desires of seeing you again.
I see the will of you
so consciously waiting
my patience cannot withhold
the thoughts of needs I have for you.
And, in silence, I reach out for a
piece of the need I've wanted for
so long.

You speak of making love to me
I close my eyes!

…Of Humankind

    Real
         ist
             ic
                 al
                     ly
                           thinking…
If the world were of freedom
and there were no doors made
to lock a man in,
                      unruly,
to cage him
                          from others who love him
if,
        one man of words,
                    would decide
to take the labels and bad names
off a man
                          to tell about humans
being inhuman,
                  Pretending they are God
To forgive, when they see
                      the consideration to forgive.

To find a power
or opposition to use as power
and debate
                    himself, so unconsciously
in other men.

Yvonne Hampden

Poem... Of Humankind

No one denies the Black Man's
Origin as being African.
No one denies the nature of Africa
as the Motherland and
      it's possible
birthplace of mankind.

No one denies Africa's soil
to be the richest of the earth.
Yet,
      the Black Man is
           continually being
held responsible
      for the common man
's appearances and dilemmas.
What it all boils down to,
      is
that,
      the common man has
held the Black Man
Responsible
      for his own existence!
For his nature, his own
life upon the Earth.
There upon,
      the common man
chooses to explore other earths,
other planets, instead of,
      first,
taking care of his own.
(We all know the earth
      to be
our natural resting place.
We were born here, nourished

and developed here, and expect
to die here).
I think his plan is to fall, off
the face of the earth.
      A suicide attempt!
Denying himself his roots (which no
plant or animal, or human can live without).
As I have been denied my roots, in the
attempt of him creating a man-made
civilization of machines and chemicals.
      A Rejection!
Of God,
    of Man,
        of mind,
            of the Universe!

Poem. . . Jan. 3rd, 1980

　　　　I know you from some
　　　　　other time and space. I know
　　　　　　that you know me. I know you do!
　　　　We've touched before, i remember. When
　　the earth was first born, and there was a no-
thingness in the atmosphere, the heavens and the
earths were one, the Universe was as fire, and smoke
filled the Air. Flames, high as the infinity of our
　reality. Gone forever, to burn away a nothingness
　　To be forever... . Gone forever, to burn away
　　　a nothingness, to tear away and soar
　　　　through the atmosphere, and to
　　　　　　divide itself amongst the
　　　　　　　clouds. To separate
　　　　　　　　me from you, i
　　　　　　　　remember.

planetary ebony

planetary ebony
the source of all human goals.
Visions
         of God-like images
taking my place in the Universe
absorbing my soul.
the black hole awaits my physical nearness
all senses erupt to sanctuary
Voices make their way
from a friction produced by
memory.
         I conceive all that is
given to me by way of consciousness.
Images force me to withhold from struggles
interrupting the calm.
All has risen to sea level
tempting to pull me back
to sea. The river attracts
the horizon + the sun surfaces as a
force forever changing the earth,
giving me a brighter day.
And if I still believe the
world is ending it's only with
the miscalculations of the
mathematics of my own mind…

Renaissance

    Dark as the night, you become
  my beginning, and my end. i want
  to create you into the image of myself.
i believe we are one image. Of one imagi-
nation that we share. The Universe
is of your color. Eyes,
as though they were stars in the night.
from head to toe i emend myself. And, for us, i
expect the same freedom to emerge from you. you see, i am
as the day. the light of darkness! i tell the world to speak
truth of your name. to dance before the daylight
hours shall dissolve you away. i speak your name
at dawn; the moon is my revelation. Dark as
your skin, within the night of your being, you remain
     as silent as you speak. to let be,
       whatever will become of me... i am
         as the day! i am
          to make a way for you. to be
           as the truth of us
            both. Together,
             we are the world!

Poem... 11/23/79

Stars shine,
          above my mind
As light in a sky
          of infinity.
I become a part of the earth.
          Earth
as a whole universe.
I hear and I see,
          And I feel
The Silence
          of the beginning!
The End of all things is Near!
people Re-awaken
          so to sleep.

Wasted days,
          wasted years.
all that's inbetween has been wasted.
Because,
          one day I lied,
to myself.
          I lied...
I lied to stay alive.

A Child of the Universe...
          Unfold into
a person of the Earth.
Unfold, into a Savior,
          for my Self!
All these years
          of me,
              being wasted
in the universe.
          I turned into a seed!

Who is God?

Who is God? I'd like to know
up above, white as the snow

Blue as the sky, round as a ball
Have mercy on me,
        and hear my call.

Dark as the night,
        bright as the sun
As powerful as life taken by a gun.

Who is God?
        A master or slave,
To life's beginning. To death's remains…

PART EIGHT

Wall to Wall

Bathing

... maybe I'd disappear
into your flesh
find a new beginning wrapped
in your warm caress...
your (dark) color would over-take
my light complexion
and my entire body would become
whole inside me.
A rush of passion would pass
through my body
memories of all the thoughts we
shared would appear.
(like a ray of affection seducing
                my presence).
I'd eat you, head to toe, and
my husband you'd become,
you see, when souls connect,
minds become one...
(like a ray of affection seducing
                my presence),
(like a ray of affection seducing
                my presence).
(like a ray of affection
bathing my presence).
(bathing my presence)
                (... bathing my presence).
(like a ray of affection bathing
                my presence).
... bathing my presence
                (in memories).

Just to be born to you!

You are my light
don't turn yourself out in my life;
in my life.
Some dark determination
that's what you are to me.
Can't describe it
words can't set it aside
definite, yet destined
to be undisguised in its
cloth of protectiveness.

You, in the likeness of God, are my love, my life,
my child, yet my death sets you apart
from all the rest.
Yes, I've died, many (of) times.
Yes, I've died, just to be born
to you,
    yes *love,*
      I've died
just to be born to you...

Yvonne Hampden

The night awaits the dawn

The night awaits the dawn
As I await your home-coming.
I frequently seek the day's light,
expecting a bird's early morning song.
The dew requests my bare
foot-steps upon its grassy enclosure.
How I'm making love to
love's blossoms...
                    ...the Godliness of you.

Michael

Michael is a Savior of my soul
His art is his love he unfolds.
Black paintings (he paints) of
Blackness to come to life.
He draws with the delight
of understanding his might.

In Black Armor, he shines
throughout the night.
Empire of galactic ecstasy
he recognizes the desires
of each patrons soul.

Ah! Michael, reach me (Michael?)
Can your paintings set me free?
Black art of my blackness
Black needs of my needs.

Michael is a savior of my soul
Michael (he) shall set free my soul
each painting with the truth it beholds
The Black painter Michael!

The Black
         the painter
                  Michael

Yvonne Hampden

My baby, Michael

Watching you
        loving every one
else but me.
          Remembering the
tenderness you left me in.
          tender moments your hands made
upon me.
      You say you want to
paint me now, but i tell you
NO! Don't paint me - love me. I
don't need to be painted,
        i need to
be loved. Not oiled on canvas or
captured in a sketch by memory,
or your frequent stares
        how dare
you!
      But, Damn you, also, for cheating
me of all you can be
    for me – of all
you can do
      together we can be one.

why'd you watch me sullenly
and remain speechless?
      Yeah, you've
forgotten about me, because when
i let your boiled eggs burn (which
is darn impossible to do), you
didn't even scold me +
      you also
didn't want to hold me (you've obviously
been with her). Igged
me all day,
      damn, all i wanted

to say, i held in
    + just stayed
as close to you as i could get.

just because we both want
    children
of our own just to born
something real we've created
from within,
    escaping into someone
else can't beat that. Nor can
it take away something real that's
for real, that you feel.
    Yeah,
i sit and wonder how
deep do you feel + wonder
why you keep saying my
fantasies can't come true, or
why you get mad if all
my dreams are of you, or if i
dream during the day,
    and don't
Awaken until it's time to sleep
Yet, i don't sleep in peace
Cause, i'm without you.
    I love you, Michael
Why should i write what
i don't feel is for real, or

write about real feelings
i don't feel.

    Yes, I want you,
baby + all my masochistic
feelings will go astray, will flow

Yvonne Hampden

away, because the hurt that that
other man caused all
      that
good-for-nothing bitterness, i
just had to split, ya know
what i mean?
      I let him go, cut
him loose - told him to rot in
hell, told him he made
my booty smell, i couldn't
stand, had, sucked my blood
gave him my heart
      now I've got to
fart him out of my life.
      Cause, baby,
i want you - i'm true,
      and I'm
gonna dread,
    get naturally read/y
for YOU - WOH!
      Yeah, baby!
i'll dig the hell out of you.
      Yeah, Michael
Stay true for me,
      all my love.

Bob Marley: A Triumph

God spoken words
sung for us to manifest
about the unrealness
of an enemy who
has chosen to possess.
And Marley knew
well of this man.
He knew his people needed a plan.
So he sung great songs
really they were warrior tunes
each note traced
for his heart to soothe.
And what was in Bob's heart
only a few will understand,
for this King's truth is being perceived
as when his music was played by his band.
And Marley is a King
his crown his people wear
people who know of the righteousness
of the sword he bared.
All illusions will pass away
those of us who believe
that Marley has gone astray.
They will see the spark
of his everlasting love. For through
his greater life of an eternal peace
he rises to the source. Moves, turns,
and rises high as the fire's flame burning
all the poison away. Burning fire in
our hearts as we watched Bob pass away.
Fools are they who don't see Bob's spirit
in us. Spoken words of he, and still a King.

Yvonne Hampden

Brothers, do your job!

Brother, hey! Brother, hey!
listen to what I've got to say,
Brother, Yeah! Brother, I mean you
watch what the brother man do.

There's a job to be done, and
we've got work to do today
Say brother, say hey!

We've got to get off our butts
and start to change our luck
with things that are holding us down
We've got work to do all over town.

Some man controlling us keeps
us back tracked, and we rebel
what we feel is the truth.
But some men who command
do it with earned pride and
demand, because the brother man
decides not to lead for truce.

Say brother, say hey!
listen to what I've got to say
Watch what the brother man do.

the therapist

THe/rapist
            trying to understand the y's
hard stick upon my
head, catching me dead between
the lies--
            I've told all i can tell
(holding my tongue),
wanting to say GO TO HELL!
            THe/rapist –charging
me on Medicaid, etc., $2.50 per pill + discharging
my spirit on Mellaril,
parading my thoughts, pondering upon my
spirit, catching me dead between the
i's of my lies. Taking me, Taking me
catching me dead, catching me dead
between the i's, taking me, taking me...
SHOT! I scream; Go Away You RAPIST!
stealing my dreams, charging me for
services undue taking up
my time, leaving me
with legs wide open, + sperm
dripping down my thighs-- my
dreams caught between my I's
suffering, suffering, drenched. . .
unaware of the real appeal
of THe/rapist, unaware of
the (reality), the suffering
caused, damn man dragged
me, muffled my face, tore
my cloth of pride, hiding
my face with an embrace
watch him, watch out for
THe/rapist -- 'Causing my dreams
of discomfort to reap out from
the penis.

Ours is a freedom world!

i submit myself to you, Michael
And when we make love
you have everything i am
i am un-
        /able to control
any part of my being, 'cause
you have every-
        thing i am,
then we become/one
one flesh, one mind-

        one
       f l e sh
       one mind
     i s u b m i t

myself to you Dear Michael
        as if you were
my God
        Waiting for you to conquer me,
to take me to new dimensions,
(drive) me to new islands/is-land
new lands, new worlds, where
every man is free
and conflict does not exist.
That's our world!
How we make love is a freedom world.

PART NINE

Back to Eden

Back to Eden

When the day ends on the moment it began,
and the earth unfolds for all its reasons.
When each child knows the other child's name,
and our hearts beat in the same season.

When we cry out for Mother Nature,
When all the day is done.
I'd take a walk with you
down by a river somewhere,
spending my time with you
right under the Sun.

like birds and butterflies

like birds and butterflies
i want to be free.
live a life forever.
life to give to you forever.
let me be a butterfly
free to give you me.
let me be a bird
I'II fly to wherever you are,
I'll fly to wherever you are.

Only butterflies are free
birds have nest and children
to feed.
Birds are dreams.
let me be a butterfly,
free to give you me.

Yvonne Hampden

To Michael with Love

There are many words
to express one thought,
one idea,
about any one thing.
But when I think of you
It's hard to express
how I feel.
Loving you, is a
poetic expression about my life.
I see through the eyes of you.
I do not need words,
or desire.
I do not need a truth or
A God,
'Cause, I have myself.
Because I have met you.
To you, Michael, with Love.
'Cause, you have been a
mirror for me.
You have
been a foresight.
I love you
as you are. . .
All my love.

Miguel

Like the bird and the fish
The air and the sea
Like a mirror is an ocean
The reality and the dream.

As Michael is Miguel
and Mikail's Navy Blue
Is a Sailor with a vision
will make *all* my dreams come true.

I row my boat down stream
A river of love I offer
'Til night and day are one again
, as we sail into forever.

I once stopped walking on my
own two feet, and sat inside a car,
You drove, I was a passenger
together we went far.

Now, in the hands of God
we've found a love so true
And, with the promise of tomorrow
I give my heart to you.

My heart is a shield,
to keep away the cold,
to block the wind of a sail,
as a sail will bring us home.

When a sea gull comes near
to eat the bait you buy
you feed him generously full
and far away he flies.

You take out your fishing pole
and you continue to fish
the ocean reflects the sun
until the tide comes in.

Yvonne Hampden

The Waiting Game

(Silence of the Lamb)

When your momma told you to diss me away,
you dissed me away,
and you played the waiting game.
You waited, yeah, you did,
While I hurt, and cried, and died up in here.
You pretended you didn't care about me for years.
Believed I would marry you, and use you
and hurt you, when deep down in your beaten heart
I was the only one who cared.
You couldn't love me, or let me go!
Then you put on a show.
The Silence of the Lamb!

Loves Face

Love has many faces, many colors, and many cares.
We cry out with needs for love
      and the answers are unclear.
Loves voice is sometimes angry,
      and sometimes bittersweet.
You quietly wait for an answer,
      and your own needs you
learn to meet.

Loves voice will tell us the secrets
within our heart and mind.
Destiny will begin with an Identity,
holding on to new life.
Need of a friend will help you turn it around.
We listen to a stranger,
and our answers are all found.

Yvonne Hampden

Epilogue

True Lover

To Miguel,

You were there that night
…I followed you with all my heart
Surrendered to the sound of your voice.

I remembered you
Because your scent aroused me…
Your eyes touched my soul.

Then, you came to me…
Free from all that changes us,
You reminded me that it's just about us.

That's why I stayed true to you
The love never died…
You are my lover, 'til the end of time…

25th Wedding Anniversary Poem

About the Reacquaintance of Love

With the courage to love again, 'The Reacquaintance of Love' walks us through the challenges of life's questionable journey. Envision the faith-filled possibilities that reflect the divine essence of the human spirit. Reflect on the many culturally diverse experiences that help us make our way in life.

About the Author

Yvonne Hampden is a native New Yorker raised in Manhattan's upper West Side (Frederick Douglas Housing Project), then near City College of New York near Sugar Hill.

As a teenager, her family relocated to the Bronx where she attended Sacred Heart of Mary High School. Graduating early, she entered the CUNY Colleges part-time, while bringing up her daughter, working occasionally to make ends meet.

With her quest to write poetry and song lyrics, she has always interacted with the community to create themes, but at the same time was considered an "individualist," someone who was shy and always on the go.

"I am so thankful for my husband, Michael Rivera, who created the nine illustrations in the book."

Yvonne Hampden lived in Yonkers, NY, from 1994 to 2013 working as a Licensed Practical Nurse. She is currently pursuing a full time career in writing. She now resides near Charlotte, North Carolina, happily married for almost 30 years.

Poetry from Adolescence to Adulthood years 1974 to 2004, 2012

www.ingramcontent.com/pod-product-compliance
Lightning Source LLC
Chambersburg PA
CBHW050559300426
44112CB00013B/1987